Reflections
In Gratitude

A Celebration Of Life's Most Fabulous Moments

This Journal Belongs To:

_____

Journal Entry Dates:

_____ to _____

Reflections In Gratitude

A Celebration Of Life's Most Fabulous Moments

Jodi Nicholson

STERLING PUBLISHING GROUP

Reflections In Gratitude
A Celebration of Life's Most Fabulous Moments

This is a work of non-fiction. This publication is designed to provide accurate information on the subject matter covered. It is sold with the understanding that the publisher is not engaged in rendering professional services or advice. The information is not intended to replace any legal council or other professional or medical directives.

Scripture quotations have been taken from the Holy Bible, NIV® Copyright by International Bible Society and any other quotations have been verified, noted and accredited to the originating author or creator.

ISBN: 978-0-9845010-1-4

Published by The Sterling Publishing Group, USA
www.SterlingPublishingGroup.com

Cover Design & Layout: Jodi Nicholson | www.JodiNicholson.com

This book may be ordered by calling: 1.888.689.1130 or 813-217-3720 or by visiting: www.AFabulousGroup.com or www.JodiNicholson.com

Printed in the United States of America

Motivational / Self Help

Journal

For the Angels ...

who sing sweetly in our dreams,

who endlessly nurture our spirit,

and who bless us so graciously.

Thank you for your love.

❤

I am grateful for the

abundant blessings of the day.

❤

Introduction

I am delighted to share with you the many gifts that accompany this book, *Reflections in Gratitude – A Celebration of Life's Most Fabulous Moments.* Thank you for choosing to live the journey and feel the joy with me in gratitude. I am truly honored.

The act of reflection is to sincerely focus on a thought, activity or some other item of importance with careful consideration. Often times this is best accomplished in a quiet space or soon after being in a calm or meditative state. This process combined with the intention centered in a state of gratitude (feeling grateful or being thankful), can evolve into a profound realization resulting in peacefulness, prosperity, joy, comfort and ultimately, pure love. This can even occur in the midst of what may appear to be a chaotic day. These are just a few words I use to describe the feelings I experience through this type of journaling. Most of all, it makes me feel simply fabulous! And to those familiar with my tagline and life's journey ... "It's Okay To Be Fabulous!" ™

I have been journaling and reflecting on my accomplishments faithfully since the age of 16. I began in 1981 by celebrating a year of accomplishments and successes on my birthday rather than celebrating my age or how "old" I was going to be. I would use my birthday to reflect on the entire year and then would set and revise my goals for the coming year. As a young woman this seemed odd to friends and family yet I found myself completely numb to their comments or concerns, even uninterested in birthday parties, celebrations or other distractions until my priorities were completed ... the many gifts I have received over the years from this activity has far outweighed any material item or event imaginable. Now, I always enjoy an amazing celebration so once the reflecting was complete, I was sure to participate in all the fun festivities.

Personally, I wake up every day the same way I go to sleep ... SMILING and full of JOY! I believe we have a choice in any situation so I choose happiness, love and kindness. I lay my head down at night with a feeling of completeness, oneness with Spirit and filled in gratitude.

I am where I am when I am supposed to be there, and for the majority of the time, I show up smiling! You see, I choose to live a joyful life in the context of peace, unity and love while being in harmony with my unique gifts (my God given gifts and talents). My life's purpose is in continuous evolution and growth as I help others prosper and inspire a vision to live in our true essence, mine being "I am poised in elegance and grace" allowing the many blessings of each day to flourish and flow effortlessly. You see for any unhappy thought there is an opposite word, meaning or feeling to counteract or counterbalance it (Yin & Yang). I choose the positive side and focus on the light, the full glass and the blessing. I wish this for you should this be your choice. I have provided a list of virtues, traits and fabulous moments to consider at the end of the journal. You may want to incorporate and adopt some of the words, phrases or meaning into your journaling. I also recommend keeping a thesaurus handy. I utilize www.thesaurus.com and when I need a positive replacement word for a not-so-fabulous word or feeling, I go in search of empowerment through positivity.

Reflections in Gratitude – A Celebration of Life's Most Fabulous Moments is a simple, clear method of journaling. There are no pre-printed days or dates so you are not bound by formalities so you can be free. Journal when you can, daily is ideal and *anytime is always the right time*. I do suggest committing to a time and making it an "appointment on your calendar," an actual commitment until it becomes natural to you like brushing your teeth. As you establish the act of journaling, embrace the "life" it brings. When something has meaning attached to it and you can immerse yourself to see, hear, feel, smell and taste the experiences, then you bring the experience depth and breath; you give it life. Focus on the outcome of the many benefits this particular journal can offer you ... It's about being thankful and grateful for whatever you choose, it's about your accomplishments, successes, and fabulous moments that you want to remember, and the reflections you have through the experience. While in reflection ask yourself, could I have done something differently? If so, then focus on the outcome with a different component added. How do you feel? Why? What's new and fabulous today? Do share ... it's fun!

Most importantly, feel free with your thoughts, feelings and expressions as you reflect, explore and enjoy the journey. When you see a positive affirmation at the bottom of a page, read it and then say the affirmation out loud. Take a deep breath, exhale and pause for a moment and allow yourself to be inspired.

After every seven entry days there is a heart symbol ❤ to remind you that you are loved. This heart is followed by a quote or message from scripture and offered as inspiration to provoke deeper thought and awareness for you to examine either in retrospect or from within. I've provided a blank space or "doodle area" just in case you want to jot down notes, thoughts or pictures ... whatever you desire. Finally, at the end of the space there is a word and a butterfly. The word represents a trait, virtue or expression and its meaning is provided in the resource section of the journal. The butterfly is to remind you about the freedom journaling brings. You are the evolution of YOU. You are in a continuous transformative state to be, do and/or become your true authentic self.

Remember, you are simply fabulous and now we can say my tagline together because ..."It's Okay To Be Fabulous!" ™

In Everlasting Gratitude,

Jodi Nicholson

❤

Jodi Nicholson is the Founder and CEO of A Fabulous Group, Inc. and Co-Founder and CEO of The Success Coach Institute. With over 25 years experience combined with her entrepreneurial spirit she specializes in Business, Marketing and Motivation for her individual and corporate clients Worldwide. She is an Author, Speaker and Master Certified Success Coach. For more information, visit: http://www.AFabulousGroup.com

I am grateful for the gifts of

honesty, truth, loyalty, faithfulness,

compassion and tenacity as I evolve

in Your endless realm of grace.

Thank you.

❤

Reflections In Gratitude

Reflecting in gratitude, thankfulness, gratefulness or appreciation is a positive emotion or attitude in acknowledging the benefit one has received or will receive. It is also a state of being and when a person embraces this quality they are grounded steadfast in its path and living in the journey that is underway.

By embracing gratitude in our life we are placed in a state of appreciation. We are thankful for each day and the events and energy created by and through our presence. By focusing on gratitude we become more aware of all aspects of life and balance, and this ultimately creates a shift in our thinking to a positive state, naturally and effortlessly. To be consciously thankful each day is to be consciously present for our selves, for others and for the Universe.

The gratitude journal is a way to appreciate, acknowledge and focus our attention to the many things we are thankful for each day. We can recognize people, events, situations, objects, nature, and ourselves through our presence in abundance and graciousness. Journaling is considered a stress reducer and can strengthen emotional resilience and awareness. By fully focusing on gratitude, reflecting on the gratitude and then writing about it builds upon our character and our unconscious conscience. It keeps us focused on the positive things in life, nurturing our spirit, allowing us to learn, grow and soar within our existence.

The daily journal begins on the next page and provides space to write about gratefulness, celebrations, fabulous moments and your own reflections; The inspirational section appears every seven days with room to jot your aha moments, quantum leaps, doodles and special thoughts; the references section follows and is inclusive of positive traits, characteristics, virtues and core values; At the end you will find a bonus section to document those extra special moments of fabulousness that have been life changing, transformational and truly inspirational for you to remember, pursue or reflect upon further. Now, it's time to live the journey and feel the joy, everyday as you *reflect in gratitude.*

Day & Date _____

I am grateful for _____

_____

_____

Celebrations _____

_____

Fabulous Moments _____

_____

Reflections _____

_____

_____

Day & Date _____

I am grateful for _____

_____

_____

Celebrations _____

_____

Fabulous Moments _____

_____

Reflections _____

_____

_____

I am joyful

Day & Date _____

I am grateful for _____

_____

_____

Celebrations _____

_____

Fabulous Moments _____

_____

Reflections _____

_____

_____

Day & Date _____

I am grateful for _____

_____

_____

Celebrations _____

_____

Fabulous Moments _____

_____

Reflections _____

_____

_____

I am empowered

Day & Date _____

I am grateful for _____

_____

_____

Celebrations _____

_____

Fabulous Moments _____

_____

Reflections _____

_____

_____

Day & Date _____

I am grateful for _____

_____

_____

Celebrations _____

_____

Fabulous Moments _____

_____

Reflections _____

_____

_____

I am love

Day & Date _____

I am grateful for _____

_____

_____

Celebrations _____

_____

Fabulous Moments _____

_____

Reflections _____

_____

_____

♥

**"Let us always meet each other with smile,
for the smile is the beginning of love."**

- Mother Teresa

Love and Joy

Day & Date _____

I am grateful for _____

_____

_____

Celebrations _____

_____

Fabulous Moments _____

_____

Reflections _____

_____

_____

Day & Date _____

I am grateful for _____

_____

_____

Celebrations _____

_____

Fabulous Moments _____

_____

Reflections _____

_____

_____

I am peaceful

Day & Date _____

I am grateful for _____

_____

_____

Celebrations _____

_____

Fabulous Moments _____

_____

Reflections _____

_____

_____

Day & Date _____

I am grateful for _____

_____

_____

Celebrations _____

_____

Fabulous Moments _____

_____

Reflections _____

_____

_____

I am authentic

Day & Date _____

I am grateful for _____

_____

_____

Celebrations _____

_____

Fabulous Moments _____

_____

Reflections _____

_____

_____

Day & Date _____

I am grateful for _____

_____

_____

Celebrations _____

_____

Fabulous Moments _____

_____

Reflections _____

_____

_____

I am beauty

Day & Date _____

I am grateful for _____

_____

_____

Celebrations _____

_____

Fabulous Moments _____

_____

Reflections _____

_____

_____

♥

**The fruit of the Spirit is love, joy, peace,
patience, kindness, goodness, faithfulness,
gentleness and self-control.**

- Galatians 5:22-23 NIV

Abundance

Day & Date _____

I am grateful for _____

_____

_____

Celebrations _____

_____

Fabulous Moments _____

_____

Reflections _____

_____

_____

Day & Date _____

I am grateful for _____

_____

_____

Celebrations _____

_____

Fabulous Moments _____

_____

Reflections _____

_____

_____

I am creative

Day & Date _____

I am grateful for _____

_____

_____

Celebrations _____

_____

Fabulous Moments _____

_____

Reflections _____

_____

_____

Day & Date _____

I am grateful for _____

_____

_____

Celebrations _____

_____

Fabulous Moments _____

_____

Reflections _____

_____

_____

I am in harmony with my purpose

Day & Date _____

I am grateful for _____

_____

_____

Celebrations _____

_____

Fabulous Moments _____

_____

Reflections _____

_____

_____

Day & Date _____

I am grateful for _____

_____

_____

Celebrations _____

_____

Fabulous Moments _____

_____

Reflections _____

_____

_____

I am decisive

Day & Date _____

I am grateful for _____

_____

_____

Celebrations _____

_____

Fabulous Moments _____

_____

Reflections _____

_____

_____

❤

**"Gratitude is not only the greatest of virtues,
but the parent to all others."**

- Cicero

Kindness

Day & Date _____

I am grateful for _____

_____

_____

Celebrations _____

_____

Fabulous Moments _____

_____

Reflections _____

_____

_____

Day & Date _____

I am grateful for _____

_____

_____

Celebrations _____

_____

Fabulous Moments _____

_____

Reflections _____

_____

_____

I am passionate

Day & Date _____

I am grateful for _____

_____

_____

Celebrations _____

_____

Fabulous Moments _____

_____

Reflections _____

_____

_____

Day & Date _____

I am grateful for _____

_____

_____

Celebrations _____

_____

Fabulous Moments _____

_____

Reflections _____

_____

_____

I am prosperous

Day & Date _____

I am grateful for _____

_____

_____

Celebrations _____

_____

Fabulous Moments _____

_____

Reflections _____

_____

_____

Day & Date _____

I am grateful for _____

_____

_____

Celebrations _____

_____

Fabulous Moments _____

_____

Reflections _____

_____

_____

I am delighted

Day & Date _____

I am grateful for _____

_____

_____

Celebrations _____

_____

Fabulous Moments _____

_____

Reflections _____

_____

_____

❤

"If you can dream it, you can do it."

- Walt Disney

Inspiration

Day & Date _____

I am grateful for _____

_____

_____

Celebrations _____

_____

Fabulous Moments _____

_____

Reflections _____

_____

_____

Day & Date _____

I am grateful for _____

_____

_____

Celebrations _____

_____

Fabulous Moments _____

_____

Reflections _____

_____

_____

I am calm

Day & Date _____

I am grateful for _____

_____

_____

Celebrations _____

_____

Fabulous Moments _____

_____

Reflections _____

_____

_____

Day & Date _____

I am grateful for _____

_____

_____

Celebrations _____

_____

Fabulous Moments _____

_____

Reflections _____

_____

_____

I am committed

Day & Date _____

I am grateful for _____

_____

_____

Celebrations _____

_____

Fabulous Moments _____

_____

Reflections _____

_____

_____

Day & Date _____

I am grateful for _____

_____

_____

Celebrations _____

_____

Fabulous Moments _____

_____

Reflections _____

_____

_____

I am balanced

Day & Date _____

I am grateful for _____

_____

_____

Celebrations _____

_____

Fabulous Moments _____

_____

Reflections _____

_____

_____

❤

"Gratitude is the memory of the heart."

- French Proverb

Compassion

Day & Date _____

I am grateful for _____

_____

_____

Celebrations _____

_____

Fabulous Moments _____

_____

Reflections _____

_____

_____

Day & Date _____

I am grateful for _____

_____

_____

Celebrations _____

_____

Fabulous Moments _____

_____

Reflections _____

_____

_____

I am organized

Day & Date _____

I am grateful for _____

_____

_____

Celebrations _____

_____

Fabulous Moments _____

_____

Reflections _____

_____

_____

Day & Date _____

I am grateful for _____

_____

_____

Celebrations _____

_____

Fabulous Moments _____

_____

Reflections _____

_____

_____

I am happy

Day & Date _____

I am grateful for _____

_____

_____

Celebrations _____

_____

Fabulous Moments _____

_____

Reflections _____

_____

_____

Day & Date _____

I am grateful for _____

_____

_____

Celebrations _____

_____

Fabulous Moments _____

_____

Reflections _____

_____

_____

I am special

Day & Date _____

I am grateful for _____

_____

_____

Celebrations _____

_____

Fabulous Moments _____

_____

Reflections _____

_____

_____

❤

"Gratitude makes sense of our past, brings peace for today, and creates a vision for tomorrow."

- Melody Beattie

Clarity

Day & Date _____

I am grateful for _____

_____

_____

Celebrations _____

_____

Fabulous Moments _____

_____

Reflections _____

_____

_____

Day & Date _____

I am grateful for _____

_____

_____

Celebrations _____

_____

Fabulous Moments _____

_____

Reflections _____

_____

_____

I am diversified

Day & Date _____

I am grateful for _____

_____

_____

Celebrations _____

_____

Fabulous Moments _____

_____

Reflections _____

_____

_____

Day & Date _____

I am grateful for _____

_____

_____

Celebrations _____

_____

Fabulous Moments _____

_____

Reflections _____

_____

_____

I am evolving

Day & Date _____

I am grateful for _____

_____

_____

Celebrations _____

_____

Fabulous Moments _____

_____

Reflections _____

_____

_____

Day & Date _____

I am grateful for _____

_____

_____

Celebrations _____

_____

Fabulous Moments _____

_____

Reflections _____

_____

_____

I am wealthy

Day & Date _____

I am grateful for _____

_____

_____

Celebrations _____

_____

Fabulous Moments _____

_____

Reflections _____

_____

_____

❤

**"Nothing is impossible,
the word itself says I'm possible!"**

- Audrey Hepburn

Hope

Day & Date _____

I am grateful for _____

_____

_____

Celebrations _____

_____

Fabulous Moments _____

_____

Reflections _____

_____

_____

Day & Date _____

I am grateful for _____

_____

_____

Celebrations _____

_____

Fabulous Moments _____

_____

Reflections _____

_____

_____

I am beauty

Day & Date _____

I am grateful for _____

_____

_____

Celebrations _____

_____

Fabulous Moments _____

_____

Reflections _____

_____

_____

Day & Date _____

I am grateful for _____

_____

_____

Celebrations _____

_____

Fabulous Moments _____

_____

Reflections _____

_____

_____

I am extraordinary

Day & Date _____

I am grateful for _____

_____

_____

Celebrations _____

_____

Fabulous Moments _____

_____

Reflections _____

_____

_____

Day & Date _____

I am grateful for _____

_____

_____

Celebrations _____

_____

Fabulous Moments _____

_____

Reflections _____

_____

_____

I am loyal

Day & Date _____

I am grateful for _____

_____

_____

Celebrations _____

_____

Fabulous Moments _____

_____

Reflections _____

_____

_____

❤

**"Happiness is not something you postpone for the future;
it is something you design for the present."**

- Jim Rohn

Gifted

Day & Date _____

I am grateful for _____

_____

_____

Celebrations _____

_____

Fabulous Moments _____

_____

Reflections _____

_____

_____

Day & Date _____

I am grateful for _____

_____

_____

Celebrations _____

_____

Fabulous Moments _____

_____

Reflections _____

_____

_____

I am brilliance

Day & Date _____

I am grateful for _____

_____

_____

Celebrations _____

_____

Fabulous Moments _____

_____

Reflections _____

_____

_____

Day & Date _____

I am grateful for _____

_____

_____

Celebrations _____

_____

Fabulous Moments _____

_____

Reflections _____

_____

_____

I am a contributor

Day & Date _____

I am grateful for _____

_____

_____

Celebrations _____

_____

Fabulous Moments _____

_____

Reflections _____

_____

_____

Day & Date _____

I am grateful for _____

_____

_____

Celebrations _____

_____

Fabulous Moments _____

_____

Reflections _____

_____

_____

I am fabulous

Day & Date _____

I am grateful for _____

_____

_____

Celebrations _____

_____

Fabulous Moments _____

_____

Reflections _____

_____

_____

♥

**"Let love and faithfulness never leave you;
write them on the tablet of your heart."**

- Proverbs 3:3 NIV

Authenticity

Day & Date _____

I am grateful for _____

_____

_____

Celebrations _____

_____

Fabulous Moments _____

_____

Reflections _____

_____

_____

Day & Date _____

I am grateful for _____

_____

_____

Celebrations _____

_____

Fabulous Moments _____

_____

Reflections _____

_____

_____

I am special

Day & Date _____

I am grateful for _____

_____

_____

Celebrations _____

_____

Fabulous Moments _____

_____

Reflections _____

_____

_____

Day & Date _____

I am grateful for _____

_____

_____

Celebrations _____

_____

Fabulous Moments _____

_____

Reflections _____

_____

_____

I am devoted

Day & Date _____

I am grateful for _____

_____

_____

Celebrations _____

_____

Fabulous Moments _____

_____

Reflections _____

_____

_____

Day & Date _____

I am grateful for _____

_____

_____

Celebrations _____

_____

Fabulous Moments _____

_____

Reflections _____

_____

_____

I am energetic

Day & Date _____

I am grateful for _____

_____

_____

Celebrations _____

_____

Fabulous Moments _____

_____

Reflections _____

_____

_____

♥

"It is one of the most beautiful compensations of this life that no man can sincerely try to help another without helping himself."

- Ralph Waldo Emerson

Benovolence

Day & Date _____

I am grateful for _____

_____

_____

Celebrations _____

_____

Fabulous Moments _____

_____

Reflections _____

_____

_____

Day & Date _____

I am grateful for _____

_____

_____

Celebrations _____

_____

Fabulous Moments _____

_____

Reflections _____

_____

_____

I am faithful

Day & Date _____

I am grateful for _____

_____

_____

Celebrations _____

_____

Fabulous Moments _____

_____

Reflections _____

_____

_____

Day & Date _____

I am grateful for _____

_____

_____

Celebrations _____

_____

Fabulous Moments _____

_____

Reflections _____

_____

_____

I am healthy

Day & Date _____

I am grateful for _____

_____

_____

Celebrations _____

_____

Fabulous Moments _____

_____

Reflections _____

_____

_____

Day & Date _____

I am grateful for _____

_____

_____

Celebrations _____

_____

Fabulous Moments _____

_____

Reflections _____

_____

_____

I am vitality

Day & Date _____

I am grateful for _____

_____

_____

Celebrations _____

_____

Fabulous Moments _____

_____

Reflections _____

_____

_____

❤

"Prayers go up and blessings come down."

- Yiddish Proverb

Faithfulness

Day & Date _____

I am grateful for _____

_____

_____

Celebrations _____

_____

Fabulous Moments _____

_____

Reflections _____

_____

_____

Day & Date _____

I am grateful for _____

_____

_____

Celebrations _____

_____

Fabulous Moments _____

_____

Reflections _____

_____

_____

I am pure

Day & Date _____

I am grateful for _____

_____

_____

Celebrations _____

_____

Fabulous Moments _____

_____

Reflections _____

_____

_____

Day & Date _____

I am grateful for _____

_____

_____

Celebrations _____

_____

Fabulous Moments _____

_____

Reflections _____

_____

_____

I am blessed

Day & Date _____

I am grateful for _____

_____

_____

Celebrations _____

_____

Fabulous Moments _____

_____

Reflections _____

_____

_____

Day & Date _____

I am grateful for _____

_____

_____

Celebrations _____

_____

Fabulous Moments _____

_____

Reflections _____

_____

_____

I am vulnerable

Day & Date _____

I am grateful for _____

_____

_____

Celebrations _____

_____

Fabulous Moments _____

_____

Reflections _____

_____

_____

❤

"A happy heart makes a cheerful face."

- Proverbs 15:13

Smile

Day & Date _____

I am grateful for _____

_____

_____

Celebrations _____

_____

Fabulous Moments _____

_____

Reflections _____

_____

_____

Day & Date _____

I am grateful for _____

_____

_____

Celebrations _____

_____

Fabulous Moments _____

_____

Reflections _____

_____

_____

I am happy

Day & Date _____

I am grateful for _____

_____

_____

Celebrations _____

_____

Fabulous Moments _____

_____

Reflections _____

_____

_____

Day & Date _____

I am grateful for _____

_____

_____

Celebrations _____

_____

Fabulous Moments _____

_____

Reflections _____

_____

_____

I am energetic

Day & Date _____

I am grateful for _____

_____

_____

Celebrations _____

_____

Fabulous Moments _____

_____

Reflections _____

_____

_____

Day & Date _____

I am grateful for _____

_____

_____

Celebrations _____

_____

Fabulous Moments _____

_____

Reflections _____

_____

_____

I am spectacular

Day & Date _____

I am grateful for _____

_____

_____

Celebrations _____

_____

Fabulous Moments _____

_____

Reflections _____

_____

_____

♥

**"The way you get meaning into your life is to devote
yourself to loving others, devote yourself to your
community around you, and devote yourself to creating
something that gives you purpose and meaning."**

- Mitch Albom

Passion

Day & Date _____

I am grateful for _____

_____

_____

Celebrations _____

_____

Fabulous Moments _____

_____

Reflections _____

_____

_____

Day & Date _____

I am grateful for _____

_____

_____

Celebrations _____

_____

Fabulous Moments _____

_____

Reflections _____

_____

_____

I am spiritual

Day & Date _____

I am grateful for _____

_____

_____

Celebrations _____

_____

Fabulous Moments _____

_____

Reflections _____

_____

_____

Day & Date _____

I am grateful for _____

_____

_____

Celebrations _____

_____

Fabulous Moments _____

_____

Reflections _____

_____

_____

I am successful

Day & Date _____

I am grateful for _____

_____

_____

Celebrations _____

_____

Fabulous Moments _____

_____

Reflections _____

_____

_____

Day & Date _____

I am grateful for _____

_____

_____

Celebrations _____

_____

Fabulous Moments _____

_____

Reflections _____

_____

_____

I am creative

Day & Date _____

I am grateful for _____

_____

_____

Celebrations _____

_____

Fabulous Moments _____

_____

Reflections _____

_____

_____

♥

**"Spread love everywhere you go.
Let no one ever come to you without leaving happier."**

- Mother Teresa

Make It A Fabulous Day

Day & Date _____

I am grateful for _____

_____

_____

Celebrations _____

_____

Fabulous Moments _____

_____

Reflections _____

_____

_____

Day & Date _____

I am grateful for _____

_____

_____

Celebrations _____

_____

Fabulous Moments _____

_____

Reflections _____

_____

_____

I am unique

Day & Date _____

I am grateful for _____

_____

_____

Celebrations _____

_____

Fabulous Moments _____

_____

Reflections _____

_____

_____

Day & Date _____

I am grateful for _____

_____

_____

Celebrations _____

_____

Fabulous Moments _____

_____

Reflections _____

_____

_____

I am gifted

Day & Date _____

I am grateful for _____

_____

_____

Celebrations _____

_____

Fabulous Moments _____

_____

Reflections _____

_____

_____

Day & Date _____

I am grateful for _____

_____

_____

Celebrations _____

_____

Fabulous Moments _____

_____

Reflections _____

_____

_____

I am peaceful

Day & Date _____

I am grateful for _____

_____

_____

Celebrations _____

_____

Fabulous Moments _____

_____

Reflections _____

_____

_____

❤

"You don't have a soul. You are a soul. You have a body."
- C.S. Lewis

Healthfulness

Day & Date _____

I am grateful for _____

_____

_____

Celebrations _____

_____

Fabulous Moments _____

_____

Reflections _____

_____

_____

Day & Date _____

I am grateful for _____

_____

_____

Celebrations _____

_____

Fabulous Moments _____

_____

Reflections _____

_____

_____

I am amazing

Day & Date _____

I am grateful for _____

_____

_____

Celebrations _____

_____

Fabulous Moments _____

_____

Reflections _____

_____

_____

Day & Date _____

I am grateful for _____

_____

_____

Celebrations _____

_____

Fabulous Moments _____

_____

Reflections _____

_____

_____

I am love

Day & Date _____

I am grateful for _____

_____

_____

Celebrations _____

_____

Fabulous Moments _____

_____

Reflections _____

_____

_____

Day & Date _____

I am grateful for _____

_____

_____

Celebrations _____

_____

Fabulous Moments _____

_____

Reflections _____

_____

_____

I am determined

Day & Date _____

I am grateful for _____

_____

_____

Celebrations _____

_____

Fabulous Moments _____

_____

Reflections _____

_____

_____

❤

"Either you run the day or the day runs you."

- Jim Rohn

Organized

Day & Date _____

I am grateful for _____

_____

_____

Celebrations _____

_____

Fabulous Moments _____

_____

Reflections _____

_____

_____

Day & Date _____

I am grateful for _____

_____

_____

Celebrations _____

_____

Fabulous Moments _____

_____

Reflections _____

_____

_____

I am bountiful

Day & Date _____

I am grateful for _____

_____

_____

Celebrations _____

_____

Fabulous Moments _____

_____

Reflections _____

_____

_____

Day & Date _____

I am grateful for _____

_____

_____

Celebrations _____

_____

Fabulous Moments _____

_____

Reflections _____

_____

_____

I am positive

Day & Date _____

I am grateful for _____

_____

_____

Celebrations _____

_____

Fabulous Moments _____

_____

Reflections _____

_____

_____

Day & Date _____

I am grateful for _____

_____

_____

Celebrations _____

_____

Fabulous Moments _____

_____

Reflections _____

_____

_____

I am accomplished

Day & Date _____

I am grateful for _____

_____

_____

Celebrations _____

_____

Fabulous Moments _____

_____

Reflections _____

_____

_____

♥

"Put your heart, mind and soul into even your smallest acts. This is the secret of success."

- Swami Sivananda

Excellence

Day & Date _____

I am grateful for _____

_____

_____

Celebrations _____

_____

Fabulous Moments _____

_____

Reflections _____

_____

_____

Day & Date _____

I am grateful for _____

_____

_____

Celebrations _____

_____

Fabulous Moments _____

_____

Reflections _____

_____

_____

I am truthful

Day & Date _____

I am grateful for _____

_____

_____

Celebrations _____

_____

Fabulous Moments _____

_____

Reflections _____

_____

_____

Day & Date _____

I am grateful for _____

_____

_____

Celebrations _____

_____

Fabulous Moments _____

_____

Reflections _____

_____

_____

I am steadfast

Day & Date _____

I am grateful for _____

_____

_____

Celebrations _____

_____

Fabulous Moments _____

_____

Reflections _____

_____

_____

Day & Date _____

I am grateful for _____

_____

_____

Celebrations _____

_____

Fabulous Moments _____

_____

Reflections _____

_____

_____

I am honest

Day & Date _____

I am grateful for _____

_____

_____

Celebrations _____

_____

Fabulous Moments _____

_____

Reflections _____

_____

_____

❤

**"You have made known to me the paths of life;
you fill me with joy in your presence."**

- Acts 2:28 NIV

Grace

Day & Date _____

I am grateful for _____

_____

_____

Celebrations _____

_____

Fabulous Moments _____

_____

Reflections _____

_____

_____

Day & Date _____

I am grateful for _____

_____

_____

Celebrations _____

_____

Fabulous Moments _____

_____

Reflections _____

_____

_____

I am dedicated

Day & Date _____

I am grateful for _____

_____

_____

Celebrations _____

_____

Fabulous Moments _____

_____

Reflections _____

_____

_____

Day & Date _____

I am grateful for _____

_____

_____

Celebrations _____

_____

Fabulous Moments _____

_____

Reflections _____

_____

_____

I am joy

Day & Date _____

I am grateful for _____

_____

_____

Celebrations _____

_____

Fabulous Moments _____

_____

Reflections _____

_____

_____

Day & Date _____

I am grateful for _____

_____

_____

Celebrations _____

_____

Fabulous Moments _____

_____

Reflections _____

_____

_____

I am peace

Day & Date _____

I am grateful for _____

_____

_____

Celebrations _____

_____

Fabulous Moments _____

_____

Reflections _____

_____

_____

❤

"You were born to win, but to be a winner, you must plan to win, prepare to win, and expect to win."

- Zig Zigler

Victory

Day & Date _____

I am grateful for _____

_____

_____

Celebrations _____

_____

Fabulous Moments _____

_____

Reflections _____

_____

_____

Day & Date _____

I am grateful for _____

_____

_____

Celebrations _____

_____

Fabulous Moments _____

_____

Reflections _____

_____

_____

I am free

Day & Date _____

I am grateful for _____

_____

_____

Celebrations _____

_____

Fabulous Moments _____

_____

Reflections _____

_____

_____

Day & Date _____

I am grateful for _____

_____

_____

Celebrations _____

_____

Fabulous Moments _____

_____

Reflections _____

_____

_____

I am the light

Day & Date _____

I am grateful for _____

_____

_____

Celebrations _____

_____

Fabulous Moments _____

_____

Reflections _____

_____

_____

Day & Date _____

I am grateful for _____

_____

_____

Celebrations _____

_____

Fabulous Moments _____

_____

Reflections _____

_____

_____

I am excellent

Day & Date _____

I am grateful for _____

_____

_____

Celebrations _____

_____

Fabulous Moments _____

_____

Reflections _____

_____

_____

❤

**"For the Lord your God will bless you,
... and your joy will be complete."**

- Deuteronomy 16:15 NIV

Perfection

Day & Date _____

I am grateful for _____

_____

_____

Celebrations _____

_____

Fabulous Moments _____

_____

Reflections _____

_____

_____

Day & Date _____

I am grateful for _____

_____

_____

Celebrations _____

_____

Fabulous Moments _____

_____

Reflections _____

_____

_____

I am balanced

Day & Date _____

I am grateful for _____

_____

_____

Celebrations _____

_____

Fabulous Moments _____

_____

Reflections _____

_____

_____

Day & Date _____

I am grateful for _____

_____

_____

Celebrations _____

_____

Fabulous Moments _____

_____

Reflections _____

_____

_____

I am innovative

Day & Date _____

I am grateful for _____

_____

_____

Celebrations _____

_____

Fabulous Moments _____

_____

Reflections _____

_____

_____

Day & Date _____

I am grateful for _____

_____

_____

Celebrations _____

_____

Fabulous Moments _____

_____

Reflections _____

_____

_____

I am loving

Day & Date _____

I am grateful for _____

_____

_____

Celebrations _____

_____

Fabulous Moments _____

_____

Reflections _____

_____

_____

❤

"He is a wise man who does not grieve for the things which he has not, but rejoices for those which he has."

- Epictetus

Day & Date _____

I am grateful for _____

_____

_____

Celebrations _____

_____

Fabulous Moments _____

_____

Reflections _____

_____

_____

Day & Date _____

I am grateful for _____

_____

_____

Celebrations _____

_____

Fabulous Moments _____

_____

Reflections _____

_____

_____

I am special

Day & Date _____

I am grateful for _____

_____

_____

Celebrations _____

_____

Fabulous Moments _____

_____

Reflections _____

_____

_____

Day & Date _____

I am grateful for _____

_____

_____

Celebrations _____

_____

Fabulous Moments _____

_____

Reflections _____

_____

_____

I am kind

Day & Date _____

I am grateful for _____

_____

_____

Celebrations _____

_____

Fabulous Moments _____

_____

Reflections _____

_____

_____

Day & Date _____

I am grateful for _____

_____

_____

Celebrations _____

_____

Fabulous Moments _____

_____

Reflections _____

_____

_____

I am caring

Day & Date _____

I am grateful for _____

_____

_____

Celebrations _____

_____

Fabulous Moments _____

_____

Reflections _____

_____

_____

❤

"Tap into Spirit; it is always faithful."

- Jodi Nicholson

Prayer

Day & Date _____

I am grateful for _____

_____

_____

Celebrations _____

_____

Fabulous Moments _____

_____

Reflections _____

_____

_____

Day & Date _____

I am grateful for _____

_____

_____

Celebrations _____

_____

Fabulous Moments _____

_____

Reflections _____

_____

_____

I am thoughtful

Day & Date _____

I am grateful for _____

_____

_____

Celebrations _____

_____

Fabulous Moments _____

_____

Reflections _____

_____

_____

Day & Date _____

I am grateful for _____

_____

_____

Celebrations _____

_____

Fabulous Moments _____

_____

Reflections _____

_____

_____

I am pretty

Day & Date _____

I am grateful for _____

_____

_____

Celebrations _____

_____

Fabulous Moments _____

_____

Reflections _____

_____

_____

Day & Date _____

I am grateful for _____

_____

_____

Celebrations _____

_____

Fabulous Moments _____

_____

Reflections _____

_____

_____

I am integrity

Day & Date _____

I am grateful for _____

_____

_____

Celebrations _____

_____

Fabulous Moments _____

_____

Reflections _____

_____

_____

❤

**"Success is a state of mind. If you want success,
start thinking of yourself as a success."**

- Dr. Joyce Brothers

Possibilities

Day & Date _____

I am grateful for _____

_____

_____

Celebrations _____

_____

Fabulous Moments _____

_____

Reflections _____

_____

_____

Day & Date _____

I am grateful for _____

_____

_____

Celebrations _____

_____

Fabulous Moments _____

_____

Reflections _____

_____

_____

I am mindful

Day & Date _____

I am grateful for _____

_____

_____

Celebrations _____

_____

Fabulous Moments _____

_____

Reflections _____

_____

_____

Day & Date _____

I am grateful for _____

_____

_____

Celebrations _____

_____

Fabulous Moments _____

_____

Reflections _____

_____

_____

I am imaginative

Day & Date _____

I am grateful for _____

_____

_____

Celebrations _____

_____

Fabulous Moments _____

_____

Reflections _____

_____

_____

Day & Date _____

I am grateful for _____

_____

_____

Celebrations _____

_____

Fabulous Moments _____

_____

Reflections _____

_____

_____

I am a visionary

Day & Date _____

I am grateful for _____

_____

_____

Celebrations _____

_____

Fabulous Moments _____

_____

Reflections _____

_____

_____

❤

**"Destiny is not a matter of chance, it is a matter of choice;
it is not a thing to be waited for, it is a thing to be achieved."**

- Winston Churchill

Action

Day & Date _____

I am grateful for _____

_____

_____

Celebrations _____

_____

Fabulous Moments _____

_____

Reflections _____

_____

_____

Day & Date _____

I am grateful for _____

_____

_____

Celebrations _____

_____

Fabulous Moments _____

_____

Reflections _____

_____

_____

I am compassion

Day & Date _____

I am grateful for _____

_____

_____

Celebrations _____

_____

Fabulous Moments _____

_____

Reflections _____

_____

_____

Day & Date _____

I am grateful for _____

_____

_____

Celebrations _____

_____

Fabulous Moments _____

_____

Reflections _____

_____

_____

I am grateful

Day & Date _____

I am grateful for _____

_____

_____

Celebrations _____

_____

Fabulous Moments _____

_____

Reflections _____

_____

_____

Day & Date _____

I am grateful for _____

_____

_____

Celebrations _____

_____

Fabulous Moments _____

_____

Reflections _____

_____

_____

I am thoughtful

Day & Date _____

I am grateful for _____

_____

_____

Celebrations _____

_____

Fabulous Moments _____

_____

Reflections _____

_____

_____

♥

"Heaven and the heaven of heavens belong to the Lord your God, the earth with all that is in it."

- Deuteronomy 10:14

Respect

Day & Date _____

I am grateful for _____

_____

_____

Celebrations _____

_____

Fabulous Moments _____

_____

Reflections _____

_____

_____

Day & Date _____

I am grateful for _____

_____

_____

Celebrations _____

_____

Fabulous Moments _____

_____

Reflections _____

_____

_____

I am generous

Day & Date _____

I am grateful for _____

_____

_____

Celebrations _____

_____

Fabulous Moments _____

_____

Reflections _____

_____

_____

Day & Date _____

I am grateful for _____

_____

_____

Celebrations _____

_____

Fabulous Moments _____

_____

Reflections _____

_____

_____

I am humbled

Day & Date _____

I am grateful for _____

_____

_____

Celebrations _____

_____

Fabulous Moments _____

_____

Reflections _____

_____

_____

Day & Date _____

I am grateful for _____

_____

_____

Celebrations _____

_____

Fabulous Moments _____

_____

Reflections _____

_____

_____

I am valued

Day & Date _____

I am grateful for _____

_____

_____

Celebrations _____

_____

Fabulous Moments _____

_____

Reflections _____

_____

_____

❤

"Imagination is the preview of life's coming attractions."

- Albert Einstein

Dream

Day & Date _____

I am grateful for _____

_____

_____

Celebrations _____

_____

Fabulous Moments _____

_____

Reflections _____

_____

_____

Day & Date _____

I am grateful for _____

_____

_____

Celebrations _____

_____

Fabulous Moments _____

_____

Reflections _____

_____

_____

I am graceful

Day & Date _____

I am grateful for _____

_____

_____

Celebrations _____

_____

Fabulous Moments _____

_____

Reflections _____

_____

_____

Day & Date _____

I am grateful for _____

_____

_____

Celebrations _____

_____

Fabulous Moments _____

_____

Reflections _____

_____

_____

I am respectful

Day & Date _____

I am grateful for _____

_____

_____

Celebrations _____

_____

Fabulous Moments _____

_____

Reflections _____

_____

_____

Day & Date _____

I am grateful for _____

_____

_____

Celebrations _____

_____

Fabulous Moments _____

_____

Reflections _____

_____

_____

I am humility

Day & Date _____

I am grateful for _____

_____

_____

Celebrations _____

_____

Fabulous Moments _____

_____

Reflections _____

_____

_____

❤

"Live the journey; feel the joy."

- Jodi Nicholson

Happiness

Day & Date _____

I am grateful for _____

_____

_____

Celebrations _____

_____

Fabulous Moments _____

_____

Reflections _____

_____

_____

Day & Date _____

I am grateful for _____

_____

_____

Celebrations _____

_____

Fabulous Moments _____

_____

Reflections _____

_____

_____

I am appreciative

Day & Date _____

I am grateful for _____

_____

_____

Celebrations _____

_____

Fabulous Moments _____

_____

Reflections _____

_____

_____

Day & Date _____

I am grateful for _____

_____

_____

Celebrations _____

_____

Fabulous Moments _____

_____

Reflections _____

_____

_____

I am prosperity

Day & Date _____

I am grateful for _____

_____

_____

Celebrations _____

_____

Fabulous Moments _____

_____

Reflections _____

_____

_____

Day & Date _____

I am grateful for _____

_____

_____

Celebrations _____

_____

Fabulous Moments _____

_____

Reflections _____

_____

_____

I am glorious

Day & Date _____

I am grateful for _____

_____

_____

Celebrations _____

_____

Fabulous Moments _____

_____

Reflections _____

_____

_____

❤

"Follow effective action with quiet reflection. From the quiet reflection will come even more effective action."

- Peter F. Drucker

Meditation

Day & Date _____

I am grateful for _____

_____

_____

Celebrations _____

_____

Fabulous Moments _____

_____

Reflections _____

_____

_____

Day & Date _____

I am grateful for _____

_____

_____

Celebrations _____

_____

Fabulous Moments _____

_____

Reflections _____

_____

_____

I am sincere

Day & Date _____

I am grateful for _____

_____

_____

Celebrations _____

_____

Fabulous Moments _____

_____

Reflections _____

_____

_____

Day & Date _____

I am grateful for _____

_____

_____

Celebrations _____

_____

Fabulous Moments _____

_____

Reflections _____

_____

_____

I am clear

Day & Date _____

I am grateful for _____

_____

_____

Celebrations _____

_____

Fabulous Moments _____

_____

Reflections _____

_____

_____

Day & Date _____

I am grateful for _____

_____

_____

Celebrations _____

_____

Fabulous Moments _____

_____

Reflections _____

_____

_____

I am smart

Day & Date _____

I am grateful for _____

_____

_____

Celebrations _____

_____

Fabulous Moments _____

_____

Reflections _____

_____

_____

❤

"For today and its blessings I owe an attitude of gratitude."

- Clarence E. Hodges

Glorious

Day & Date _____

I am grateful for _____

_____

_____

Celebrations _____

_____

Fabulous Moments _____

_____

Reflections _____

_____

_____

Day & Date _____

I am grateful for _____

_____

_____

Celebrations _____

_____

Fabulous Moments _____

_____

Reflections _____

_____

_____

I am confident

Day & Date _____

I am grateful for _____

_____

_____

Celebrations _____

_____

Fabulous Moments _____

_____

Reflections _____

_____

_____

Day & Date _____

I am grateful for _____

_____

_____

Celebrations _____

_____

Fabulous Moments _____

_____

Reflections _____

_____

_____

I am kindhearted

Day & Date _____

I am grateful for _____

_____

_____

Celebrations _____

_____

Fabulous Moments _____

_____

Reflections _____

_____

_____

Day & Date _____

I am grateful for _____

_____

_____

Celebrations _____

_____

Fabulous Moments _____

_____

Reflections _____

_____

_____

I believe

Day & Date _____

I am grateful for _____

_____

_____

Celebrations _____

_____

Fabulous Moments _____

_____

Reflections _____

_____

_____

❤

"He who refreshes others will himself be refreshed."

- Proverbs 11:25 NIV

Bountiful

Day & Date _____

I am grateful for _____

_____

_____

Celebrations _____

_____

Fabulous Moments _____

_____

Reflections _____

_____

_____

Day & Date _____

I am grateful for _____

_____

_____

Celebrations _____

_____

Fabulous Moments _____

_____

Reflections _____

_____

_____

I am abundance

Day & Date _____

I am grateful for _____

_____

_____

Celebrations _____

_____

Fabulous Moments _____

_____

Reflections _____

_____

_____

Day & Date _____

I am grateful for _____

_____

_____

Celebrations _____

_____

Fabulous Moments _____

_____

Reflections _____

_____

_____

I am great

Day & Date _____

I am grateful for _____

_____

_____

Celebrations _____

_____

Fabulous Moments _____

_____

Reflections _____

_____

_____

Day & Date _____

I am grateful for _____

_____

_____

Celebrations _____

_____

Fabulous Moments _____

_____

Reflections _____

_____

_____

I am imaginative

Day & Date _____

I am grateful for _____

_____

_____

Celebrations _____

_____

Fabulous Moments _____

_____

Reflections _____

_____

_____

❤

**"Your hopes, dreams and ideas are like precious gems;
so be sure to polish, perfect and cherish them."**

- Jodi Nicholson

Beautiful

Day & Date _____

I am grateful for _____

_____

_____

Celebrations _____

_____

Fabulous Moments _____

_____

Reflections _____

_____

_____

Day & Date _____

I am grateful for _____

_____

_____

Celebrations _____

_____

Fabulous Moments _____

_____

Reflections _____

_____

_____

I am honored

Day & Date _____

I am grateful for _____

_____

_____

Celebrations _____

_____

Fabulous Moments _____

_____

Reflections _____

_____

_____

Day & Date _____

I am grateful for _____

_____

_____

Celebrations _____

_____

Fabulous Moments _____

_____

Reflections _____

_____

_____

I am cherishing

Day & Date _____

I am grateful for _____

_____

_____

Celebrations _____

_____

Fabulous Moments _____

_____

Reflections _____

_____

_____

Day & Date _____

I am grateful for _____

_____

_____

Celebrations _____

_____

Fabulous Moments _____

_____

Reflections _____

_____

_____

I am courageous

Day & Date _____

I am grateful for _____

_____

_____

Celebrations _____

_____

Fabulous Moments _____

_____

Reflections _____

_____

_____

❤

"Gratitude takes three forms; a feeling in the heart, an expression in words, and a giving in return."

- John Wanamaker

Valued

Day & Date _____

I am grateful for _____

_____

_____

Celebrations _____

_____

Fabulous Moments _____

_____

Reflections _____

_____

_____

Day & Date _____

I am grateful for _____

_____

_____

Celebrations _____

_____

Fabulous Moments _____

_____

Reflections _____

_____

_____

I am confident

Day & Date _____

I am grateful for _____

_____

_____

Celebrations _____

_____

Fabulous Moments _____

_____

Reflections _____

_____

_____

Day & Date _____

I am grateful for _____

_____

_____

Celebrations _____

_____

Fabulous Moments _____

_____

Reflections _____

_____

_____

I am love

Day & Date _____

I am grateful for _____

_____

_____

Celebrations _____

_____

Fabulous Moments _____

_____

Reflections _____

_____

_____

Day & Date _____

I am grateful for _____

_____

_____

Celebrations _____

_____

Fabulous Moments _____

_____

Reflections _____

_____

_____

I am intelligent

Day & Date _____

I am grateful for _____

_____

_____

Celebrations _____

_____

Fabulous Moments _____

_____

Reflections _____

_____

_____

❤

**"Each moment a blessing of abundance,
each breath a prayer of thanksgiving."**

- Michael Rawls

Gratefulness

Day & Date _____

I am grateful for _____

_____

_____

Celebrations _____

_____

Fabulous Moments _____

_____

Reflections _____

_____

_____

Day & Date _____

I am grateful for _____

_____

_____

Celebrations _____

_____

Fabulous Moments _____

_____

Reflections _____

_____

_____

I am smiling

Day & Date _____

I am grateful for _____

_____

_____

Celebrations _____

_____

Fabulous Moments _____

_____

Reflections _____

_____

_____

Day & Date _____

I am grateful for _____

_____

_____

Celebrations _____

_____

Fabulous Moments _____

_____

Reflections _____

_____

_____

I am happy

Day & Date _____

I am grateful for _____

_____

_____

Celebrations _____

_____

Fabulous Moments _____

_____

Reflections _____

_____

_____

Day & Date _____

I am grateful for _____

_____

_____

Celebrations _____

_____

Fabulous Moments _____

_____

Reflections _____

_____

_____

I am beauty

Day & Date _____

I am grateful for _____

_____

_____

Celebrations _____

_____

Fabulous Moments _____

_____

Reflections _____

_____

_____

❤

**"When eating fruit, give thanks
to the person who planted the tree."**

- Vietnamese Proverb

Plentiful

Day & Date _____

I am grateful for _____

_____

_____

Celebrations _____

_____

Fabulous Moments _____

_____

Reflections _____

_____

_____

Day & Date _____

I am grateful for _____

_____

_____

Celebrations _____

_____

Fabulous Moments _____

_____

Reflections _____

_____

_____

I am blessed

Day & Date _____

I am grateful for _____

_____

_____

Celebrations _____

_____

Fabulous Moments _____

_____

Reflections _____

_____

_____

Day & Date _____

I am grateful for _____

_____

_____

Celebrations _____

_____

Fabulous Moments _____

_____

Reflections _____

_____

_____

I am joyfull

Day & Date _____

I am grateful for _____

_____

_____

Celebrations _____

_____

Fabulous Moments _____

_____

Reflections _____

_____

_____

Day & Date _____

I am grateful for _____

_____

_____

Celebrations _____

_____

Fabulous Moments _____

_____

Reflections _____

_____

_____

I am fabulous

Day & Date _____

I am grateful for _____

_____

_____

Celebrations _____

_____

Fabulous Moments _____

_____

Reflections _____

_____

_____

❤

**"Talent is God given. Be humble. Fame is man-given.
Be grateful. Conceit is self-given. Be careful."**

- John Wooden

Humility

Day & Date _____

I am grateful for _____

_____

_____

Celebrations _____

_____

Fabulous Moments _____

_____

Reflections _____

_____

_____

Day & Date _____

I am grateful for _____

_____

_____

Celebrations _____

_____

Fabulous Moments _____

_____

Reflections _____

_____

_____

I am energized

Day & Date _____

I am grateful for _____

_____

_____

Celebrations _____

_____

Fabulous Moments _____

_____

Reflections _____

_____

_____

Day & Date _____

I am grateful for _____

_____

_____

Celebrations _____

_____

Fabulous Moments _____

_____

Reflections _____

_____

_____

I am faithful

Day & Date _____

I am grateful for _____

_____

_____

Celebrations _____

_____

Fabulous Moments _____

_____

Reflections _____

_____

_____

Day & Date _____

I am grateful for _____

_____

_____

Celebrations _____

_____

Fabulous Moments _____

_____

Reflections _____

_____

_____

I am spiritual

Day & Date _____

I am grateful for _____

_____

_____

Celebrations _____

_____

Fabulous Moments _____

_____

Reflections _____

_____

_____

♥

"No duty is more urgent than that of returning thanks."

- Saint Ambrose

Thanksgiving

Day & Date _____

I am grateful for _____

_____

_____

Celebrations _____

_____

Fabulous Moments _____

_____

Reflections _____

_____

_____

Day & Date _____

I am grateful for _____

_____

_____

Celebrations _____

_____

Fabulous Moments _____

_____

Reflections _____

_____

_____

I am funny

Day & Date _____

I am grateful for _____

_____

_____

Celebrations _____

_____

Fabulous Moments _____

_____

Reflections _____

_____

_____

Day & Date _____

I am grateful for _____

_____

_____

Celebrations _____

_____

Fabulous Moments _____

_____

Reflections _____

_____

_____

I am adventurous

Day & Date _____

I am grateful for _____

_____

_____

Celebrations _____

_____

Fabulous Moments _____

_____

Reflections _____

_____

_____

Day & Date _____

I am grateful for _____

_____

_____

Celebrations _____

_____

Fabulous Moments _____

_____

Reflections _____

_____

_____

I am kindhearted

Day & Date _____

I am grateful for _____

_____

_____

Celebrations _____

_____

Fabulous Moments _____

_____

Reflections _____

_____

_____

❤

**And the Lord said,
"I will cause all my goodness to pass in front of you."**

- Exodus 33:19 NIV

Truthfulness

Day & Date _____

I am grateful for _____

_____

_____

Celebrations _____

_____

Fabulous Moments _____

_____

Reflections _____

_____

_____

Day & Date _____

I am grateful for _____

_____

_____

Celebrations _____

_____

Fabulous Moments _____

_____

Reflections _____

_____

_____

I am gifted

Day & Date _____

I am grateful for _____

_____

_____

Celebrations _____

_____

Fabulous Moments _____

_____

Reflections _____

_____

_____

Day & Date _____

I am grateful for _____

_____

_____

Celebrations _____

_____

Fabulous Moments _____

_____

Reflections _____

_____

_____

I am special

Day & Date _____

I am grateful for _____

_____

_____

Celebrations _____

_____

Fabulous Moments _____

_____

Reflections _____

_____

_____

Day & Date _____

I am grateful for _____

_____

_____

Celebrations _____

_____

Fabulous Moments _____

_____

Reflections _____

_____

_____

I am peaceful

Day & Date _____

I am grateful for _____

_____

_____

Celebrations _____

_____

Fabulous Moments _____

_____

Reflections _____

_____

_____

❤

**"A grateful person can see and appreciate
the perfection that lies within every imperfection."**

- Jodi Nicholson

Appreciation

Day & Date _____

I am grateful for _____

_____

_____

Celebrations _____

_____

Fabulous Moments _____

_____

Reflections _____

_____

_____

Day & Date _____

I am grateful for _____

_____

_____

Celebrations _____

_____

Fabulous Moments _____

_____

Reflections _____

_____

_____

I am hopeful

Day & Date _____

I am grateful for _____

_____

_____

Celebrations _____

_____

Fabulous Moments _____

_____

Reflections _____

_____

_____

Day & Date _____

I am grateful for _____

_____

_____

Celebrations _____

_____

Fabulous Moments _____

_____

Reflections _____

_____

_____

I am inspired

Day & Date _____

I am grateful for _____

_____

_____

Celebrations _____

_____

Fabulous Moments _____

_____

Reflections _____

_____

_____

Day & Date _____

I am grateful for _____

_____

_____

Celebrations _____

_____

Fabulous Moments _____

_____

Reflections _____

_____

_____

I am action—oriented

Day & Date _____

I am grateful for _____

_____

_____

Celebrations _____

_____

Fabulous Moments _____

_____

Reflections _____

_____

_____

❤

"Live with passion."

- Tony Robbins

Day & Date _____

I am grateful for _____

_____

_____

Celebrations _____

_____

Fabulous Moments _____

_____

Reflections _____

_____

_____

Day & Date _____

I am grateful for _____

_____

_____

Celebrations _____

_____

Fabulous Moments _____

_____

Reflections _____

_____

_____

I am virtuous

Day & Date _____

I am grateful for _____

_____

_____

Celebrations _____

_____

Fabulous Moments _____

_____

Reflections _____

_____

_____

Day & Date _____

I am grateful for _____

_____

_____

Celebrations _____

_____

Fabulous Moments _____

_____

Reflections _____

_____

_____

I am a contribution

Day & Date _____

I am grateful for _____

_____

_____

Celebrations _____

_____

Fabulous Moments _____

_____

Reflections _____

_____

_____

Day & Date _____

I am grateful for _____

_____

_____

Celebrations _____

_____

Fabulous Moments _____

_____

Reflections _____

_____

_____

I am proactive

Day & Date _____

I am grateful for _____

_____

_____

Celebrations _____

_____

Fabulous Moments _____

_____

Reflections _____

_____

_____

❤

"There is no such thing as a small success."

- Kevin Klimowski

Celebrate

Day & Date _____

I am grateful for _____

_____

_____

Celebrations _____

_____

Fabulous Moments _____

_____

Reflections _____

_____

_____

Day & Date _____

I am grateful for _____

_____

_____

Celebrations _____

_____

Fabulous Moments _____

_____

Reflections _____

_____

_____

I am proud

Day & Date _____

I am grateful for _____

_____

_____

Celebrations _____

_____

Fabulous Moments _____

_____

Reflections _____

_____

_____

Day & Date _____

I am grateful for _____

_____

_____

Celebrations _____

_____

Fabulous Moments _____

_____

Reflections _____

_____

_____

I am honorable

Day & Date _____

I am grateful for _____

_____

_____

Celebrations _____

_____

Fabulous Moments _____

_____

Reflections _____

_____

_____

Day & Date _____

I am grateful for _____

_____

_____

Celebrations _____

_____

Fabulous Moments _____

_____

Reflections _____

_____

_____

I am loving

Day & Date _____

I am grateful for _____

_____

_____

Celebrations _____

_____

Fabulous Moments _____

_____

Reflections _____

_____

_____

❤

**"Choosing to be positive and having a grateful attitude is
going to determine how you're going to live your life."**

- Joel Olsteen

Determination

Day & Date _____

I am grateful for _____

_____

_____

Celebrations _____

_____

Fabulous Moments _____

_____

Reflections _____

_____

_____

Day & Date _____

I am grateful for _____

_____

_____

Celebrations _____

_____

Fabulous Moments _____

_____

Reflections _____

_____

_____

I am organized

Day & Date _____

I am grateful for _____

_____

_____

Celebrations _____

_____

Fabulous Moments _____

_____

Reflections _____

_____

_____

Day & Date _____

I am grateful for _____

_____

_____

Celebrations _____

_____

Fabulous Moments _____

_____

Reflections _____

_____

_____

I am considerate

Day & Date _____

I am grateful for _____

_____

_____

Celebrations _____

_____

Fabulous Moments _____

_____

Reflections _____

_____

_____

Day & Date _____

I am grateful for _____

_____

_____

Celebrations _____

_____

Fabulous Moments _____

_____

Reflections _____

_____

_____

I am healthy

Day & Date _____

I am grateful for _____

_____

_____

Celebrations _____

_____

Fabulous Moments _____

_____

Reflections _____

_____

_____

❤

**"A simple grateful thought turned heavenwards
is the most perfect prayer."**

- Doris Lessing

Humbling

Day & Date _____

I am grateful for _____

_____

_____

Celebrations _____

_____

Fabulous Moments _____

_____

Reflections _____

_____

_____

Day & Date _____

I am grateful for _____

_____

_____

Celebrations _____

_____

Fabulous Moments _____

_____

Reflections _____

_____

_____

I am fortunate

Day & Date _____

I am grateful for _____

_____

_____

Celebrations _____

_____

Fabulous Moments _____

_____

Reflections _____

_____

_____

Day & Date _____

I am grateful for _____

_____

_____

Celebrations _____

_____

Fabulous Moments _____

_____

Reflections _____

_____

_____

I am patient

Day & Date _____

I am grateful for _____

_____

_____

Celebrations _____

_____

Fabulous Moments _____

_____

Reflections _____

_____

_____

Day & Date _____

I am grateful for _____

_____

_____

Celebrations _____

_____

Fabulous Moments _____

_____

Reflections _____

_____

_____

I am conscientious

Day & Date _____

I am grateful for _____

_____

_____

Celebrations _____

_____

Fabulous Moments _____

_____

Reflections _____

_____

_____

♥

**"As we express our gratitude,
we must never forget that the highest appreciation
is not to utter words, but to live by them."**

- John F. Kennedy

Integrity

Day & Date _____

I am grateful for _____

_____

_____

Celebrations _____

_____

Fabulous Moments _____

_____

Reflections _____

_____

_____

Day & Date _____

I am grateful for _____

_____

_____

Celebrations _____

_____

Fabulous Moments _____

_____

Reflections _____

_____

_____

I am excellent

Day & Date _____

I am grateful for _____

_____

_____

Celebrations _____

_____

Fabulous Moments _____

_____

Reflections _____

_____

_____

Day & Date _____

I am grateful for _____

_____

_____

Celebrations _____

_____

Fabulous Moments _____

_____

Reflections _____

_____

_____

I am trustworthy

Day & Date _____

I am grateful for _____

_____

_____

Celebrations _____

_____

Fabulous Moments _____

_____

Reflections _____

_____

_____

Day & Date _____

I am grateful for _____

_____

_____

Celebrations _____

_____

Fabulous Moments _____

_____

Reflections _____

_____

_____

I am love

Day & Date _____

I am grateful for _____

_____

_____

Celebrations _____

_____

Fabulous Moments _____

_____

Reflections _____

_____

_____

♥

**"Thousands of candles can be lit from a single candle,
and the life of the candle will not be shortened.
Happiness never decreases by being shared."**

- Buddha

Generosity

Day & Date _____

I am grateful for _____

_____

_____

Celebrations _____

_____

Fabulous Moments _____

_____

Reflections _____

_____

_____

Day & Date _____

I am grateful for _____

_____

_____

Celebrations _____

_____

Fabulous Moments _____

_____

Reflections _____

_____

_____

I am creative

Day & Date _____

I am grateful for _____

_____

_____

Celebrations _____

_____

Fabulous Moments _____

_____

Reflections _____

_____

_____

Day & Date _____

I am grateful for _____

_____

_____

Celebrations _____

_____

Fabulous Moments _____

_____

Reflections _____

_____

_____

I am special

Day & Date _____

I am grateful for _____

_____

_____

Celebrations _____

_____

Fabulous Moments _____

_____

Reflections _____

_____

_____

Day & Date _____

I am grateful for _____

_____

_____

Celebrations _____

_____

Fabulous Moments _____

_____

Reflections _____

_____

_____

I am receptive

Day & Date _____

I am grateful for _____

_____

_____

Celebrations _____

_____

Fabulous Moments _____

_____

Reflections _____

_____

_____

❤

"They may forget what you said but they will never forget how you made them feel."

- Carl W. Buechner

Kindheartedness

Day & Date _____

I am grateful for _____

_____

_____

Celebrations _____

_____

Fabulous Moments _____

_____

Reflections _____

_____

_____

Day & Date _____

I am grateful for _____

_____

_____

Celebrations _____

_____

Fabulous Moments _____

_____

Reflections _____

_____

_____

I am prepared

Day & Date _____

I am grateful for _____

_____

_____

Celebrations _____

_____

Fabulous Moments _____

_____

Reflections _____

_____

_____

Day & Date _____

I am grateful for _____

_____

_____

Celebrations _____

_____

Fabulous Moments _____

_____

Reflections _____

_____

_____

I am sweet

Day & Date _____

I am grateful for _____

_____

_____

Celebrations _____

_____

Fabulous Moments _____

_____

Reflections _____

_____

_____

Day & Date _____

I am grateful for _____

_____

_____

Celebrations _____

_____

Fabulous Moments _____

_____

Reflections _____

_____

_____

I am peaceful

Day & Date _____

I am grateful for _____

_____

_____

Celebrations _____

_____

Fabulous Moments _____

_____

Reflections _____

_____

_____

❤

**"The future belongs to those who
believe in the beauty of their dreams."**

- Eleanor Roosevelt

Imagination

Day & Date _____

I am grateful for _____

_____

_____

Celebrations _____

_____

Fabulous Moments _____

_____

Reflections _____

_____

_____

Day & Date _____

I am grateful for _____

_____

_____

Celebrations _____

_____

Fabulous Moments _____

_____

Reflections _____

_____

_____

I am thoughtful

Day & Date _____

I am grateful for _____

_____

_____

Celebrations _____

_____

Fabulous Moments _____

_____

Reflections _____

_____

_____

Day & Date _____

I am grateful for _____

_____

_____

Celebrations _____

_____

Fabulous Moments _____

_____

Reflections _____

_____

_____

I am incredible

Day & Date _____

I am grateful for _____

_____

_____

Celebrations _____

_____

Fabulous Moments _____

_____

Reflections _____

_____

_____

Day & Date _____

I am grateful for _____

_____

_____

Celebrations _____

_____

Fabulous Moments _____

_____

Reflections _____

_____

_____

I am magnificent

Day & Date _____

I am grateful for _____

_____

_____

Celebrations _____

_____

Fabulous Moments _____

_____

Reflections _____

_____

_____

❤

"Write injuries in dust and benefits in marble ."

- Benjamin Franklin

Legacy

Day & Date _____

I am grateful for _____

_____

_____

Celebrations _____

_____

Fabulous Moments _____

_____

Reflections _____

_____

_____

Day & Date _____

I am grateful for _____

_____

_____

Celebrations _____

_____

Fabulous Moments _____

_____

Reflections _____

_____

_____

I am groovy

Day & Date _____

I am grateful for _____

_____

_____

Celebrations _____

_____

Fabulous Moments _____

_____

Reflections _____

_____

_____

Day & Date _____

I am grateful for _____

_____

_____

Celebrations _____

_____

Fabulous Moments _____

_____

Reflections _____

_____

_____

I am admirable

Day & Date _____

I am grateful for _____

_____

_____

Celebrations _____

_____

Fabulous Moments _____

_____

Reflections _____

_____

_____

Day & Date _____

I am grateful for _____

_____

_____

Celebrations _____

_____

Fabulous Moments _____

_____

Reflections _____

_____

_____

I am fascinating

Day & Date _____

I am grateful for _____

_____

_____

Celebrations _____

_____

Fabulous Moments _____

_____

Reflections _____

_____

_____

❤

**"The best and most beautiful things
in the world cannot be seen or even touched –
they must be felt with the heart."**

- Helen Keller

Believing

Day & Date _____

I am grateful for _____

_____

_____

Celebrations _____

_____

Fabulous Moments _____

_____

Reflections _____

_____

_____

Day & Date _____

I am grateful for _____

_____

_____

Celebrations _____

_____

Fabulous Moments _____

_____

Reflections _____

_____

_____

I am confident

Day & Date _____

I am grateful for _____

_____

_____

Celebrations _____

_____

Fabulous Moments _____

_____

Reflections _____

_____

_____

Day & Date _____

I am grateful for _____

_____

_____

Celebrations _____

_____

Fabulous Moments _____

_____

Reflections _____

_____

_____

I am expressive

Day & Date _____

I am grateful for _____

_____

_____

Celebrations _____

_____

Fabulous Moments _____

_____

Reflections _____

_____

_____

Day & Date _____

I am grateful for _____

_____

_____

Celebrations _____

_____

Fabulous Moments _____

_____

Reflections _____

_____

_____

I am fantastic

Day & Date _____

I am grateful for _____

_____

_____

Celebrations _____

_____

Fabulous Moments _____

_____

Reflections _____

_____

_____

❤

**"Go confidently in the direction of your dreams.
Live the life you have imagined."**

- Henry David Thoreau

Vision

Day & Date _____

I am grateful for _____

_____

_____

Celebrations _____

_____

Fabulous Moments _____

_____

Reflections _____

_____

_____

Day & Date _____

I am grateful for _____

_____

_____

Celebrations _____

_____

Fabulous Moments _____

_____

Reflections _____

_____

_____

I am cordial

Day & Date _____

I am grateful for _____

_____

_____

Celebrations _____

_____

Fabulous Moments _____

_____

Reflections _____

_____

_____

Day & Date _____

I am grateful for _____

_____

_____

Celebrations _____

_____

Fabulous Moments _____

_____

Reflections _____

_____

_____

I am reverent

Day & Date _____

I am grateful for _____

_____

_____

Celebrations _____

_____

Fabulous Moments _____

_____

Reflections _____

_____

_____

Day & Date _____

I am grateful for _____

_____

_____

Celebrations _____

_____

Fabulous Moments _____

_____

Reflections _____

_____

_____

I am warm—hearted

Day & Date _____

I am grateful for _____

_____

_____

Celebrations _____

_____

Fabulous Moments _____

_____

Reflections _____

_____

_____

❤

"How beautiful a day can be when kindness touches it!"

- George Elliston

Peacefulness

Day & Date _____

I am grateful for _____

_____

_____

Celebrations _____

_____

Fabulous Moments _____

_____

Reflections _____

_____

_____

Day & Date _____

I am grateful for _____

_____

_____

Celebrations _____

_____

Fabulous Moments _____

_____

Reflections _____

_____

_____

I am considerate

Day & Date _____

I am grateful for _____

_____

_____

Celebrations _____

_____

Fabulous Moments _____

_____

Reflections _____

_____

_____

Day & Date _____

I am grateful for _____

_____

_____

Celebrations _____

_____

Fabulous Moments _____

_____

Reflections _____

_____

_____

I am joy

Day & Date _____

I am grateful for _____

_____

_____

Celebrations _____

_____

Fabulous Moments _____

_____

Reflections _____

_____

_____

Day & Date _____

I am grateful for _____

_____

_____

Celebrations _____

_____

Fabulous Moments _____

_____

Reflections _____

_____

_____

I am amicable

Day & Date _____

I am grateful for _____

_____

_____

Celebrations _____

_____

Fabulous Moments _____

_____

Reflections _____

_____

_____

❤

**"Look lovingly upon the present,
for it holds the only things that are forever true."**

- A Course In Miracles

Blessings

Day & Date _____

I am grateful for _____

_____

_____

Celebrations _____

_____

Fabulous Moments _____

_____

Reflections _____

_____

_____

Day & Date _____

I am grateful for _____

_____

_____

Celebrations _____

_____

Fabulous Moments _____

_____

Reflections _____

_____

_____

I am empathetic

Day & Date _____

I am grateful for _____

_____

_____

Celebrations _____

_____

Fabulous Moments _____

_____

Reflections _____

_____

_____

Day & Date _____

I am grateful for _____

_____

_____

Celebrations _____

_____

Fabulous Moments _____

_____

Reflections _____

_____

_____

I am special

Day & Date _____

I am grateful for _____

_____

_____

Celebrations _____

_____

Fabulous Moments _____

_____

Reflections _____

_____

_____

Day & Date _____

I am grateful for _____

_____

_____

Celebrations _____

_____

Fabulous Moments _____

_____

Reflections _____

_____

_____

I am lovable

Day & Date _____

I am grateful for _____

_____

_____

Celebrations _____

_____

Fabulous Moments _____

_____

Reflections _____

_____

_____

❤

"Just as each one has received a gift, use it to serve one another as good stewards of the manifold grace of God."

- 1 Peter 4:10

Purposeful

♥

"Develop an attitude of gratitude,
and give thanks for everything that happens to you,
knowing that every step forward
is a step toward achieving something
bigger and better than your current situation."

- Brian Tracy

 Mindfulness

Resources

♥

Fabulous Words, Virtues and Values!

Abundance, Abundant, Abundantly - *an extremely plentiful or an over-sufficient quantity; overflowing fullness: abundance of the heart; affluence; wealth: the enjoyment of abundance; present in great quantity; more than adequate; richly supplied.*

Accomplished, Accomplishments – *having all the social graces, manners and other attainments of politeness; highly skilled; an expert; completed; done; to bring to completion a goal or conclusion; to finish; completeness; fulfilled.*

Action-Oriented – *to bring about action to completion; put things into position and order; survey things into a specified direction to completion.*

Admirable – *worthy of admiration, praises, approval, reverence or affection; excellent; first rate; prime.*

Adventurous – *inclined or willing to engage in adventure; enjoying adventures; possessing courage to participate in an adventure. An adventure is an exciting or unusual experience. One can be adventurous without placing themselves in danger or at risk.*

Amazing – *awe-inspiring, awesome, astonishing; to be surprised in sudden wonder; to be delighted or to bring about delight; a delightful experience.*

Amicable – *friendly; showing goodwill, peaceable; agreeable.*

Appreciate, Appreciated, Appreciation, Appreciative – *gratitude; thankful recognition; giving a clear perception or recognition (of value); feeling or showing appreciation and recognition.*

Authentic – *genuine; real; not false or copied; verified and supported by unquestionable evidence; reliable; trustworthy.*

Balanced – *being in harmonious or proper proportion; fair; equitable; just.*

Beautiful, Beauty – *having qualities that give great pleasure to the senses (see, hear, think, smell, feel); Excellence of its kind; wonderful; pleasing; satisfying; fantastic; extraordinary; incredible; Beauty is the quality present in a person or thing that gives intense pleasure to the mind, whether arising from sensory manifestations, design or personality in which high spiritual qualities manifest.*

Believe – *to have confidence in the truth, existence or reliability in something or someone without absolute proof; credence; conviction; to have trust and faith in benevolence, honesty and reliability.*

Benevolence – *goodwill; charitableness; an act of kindness; desire to bring goodwill and contribution.*

Blessed – *sacred; consecrated; holy; worthy of adoration; fortunate; divinely favored; blissfully happy and content; bringing happiness and thankfulness.*

Bountiful – *abundant; ample; generous; liberal in bestowing gifts; plentiful.*

Brilliance – *great brightness; excellence; magnificence; radiant; distinct.*

Calm – *tranquil; stillness; freedom from agitation; serene; still.*

Caring – *to watch over or attend to others and things with concern; to have an inclination, liking, affection or fondness for others and things.*

Celebrate, Celebration – *to commemorate an event or observe a day with festivities; to proclaim success; to praise favorably; to acknowledge joyfully.*

Cheerful – *in good spirits; pleasant; hearty; full of cheer – a shout of encouragement, approval, congratulations and enthusiasm that gives joy or gladness or gaiety.*

Cherishing – *to hold and treat something or someone dearly; feel love; care for tenderly; nurture and nurturing; to treat with value and strength affectionately with kindness; valuable.*

Clarity, Clear, Clearness - *clearness in understanding and perception; lucidity; freedom from ambiguity; having distinction; the state of being clear is to be understood easily; without blemish; transparent; concise.*

Committed – *to give in trust; to pledge oneself; to bind or obligate; to bind to a promise; to entrust for safekeeping; to engage in the highest standards.*

Compassion – *the feeling of deep sympathy for another during any misfortune accompanied by the strong desire to alleviate any of their pain or suffering; merciful; tender; commiseration; a favorable or approving accord.*

Concise – *expressing much in just a few words; to briefly cover something in a comprehensive manner, succinctly and with clarity and preciseness.*

Confidence, Confident – *sure of oneself with assurance and strong belief; certainty; successfulness; bold and secure; trustful. Also associated with being a confidant – a close friend or associate to whom secrets can be shared, confided and whom private matters are discussed and contained.*

Conscientious – *controlled by or done according to one conscience; scrupulous; meticulous; just; upright; honest; faithful; devoted; dedicated. Conscience is the inner sense of what is right and wrong in a persons motives, conduct, acts, principles impelling one towards right action. The complex of ethical and moral principles controlling the thoughts and actions of an individual. To be ethically and morally intact for the good, fair and just.*

Considerate – *the act of showing kind regard and awareness for anther person's feelings; kind; patient; concerned.*

Contribution – *the act of contributing or giving assistance, knowledge, time, money or charity. To be an important fact in helping others, a cause or a charity. To give charitably.*

Cordial – *to be gracious, amicable, courteous, friendly, warm, sincere, heartfelt; to be invigorating or exhilarating in gratitude.*

Courageous – *brave, to have courage – the quality of mind or spirit that enables a person to face anything without fear; fearlessness even in the midst of danger, pain or difficulty. Courage in conviction is to act in accordance with one's beliefs regardless of criticism; heroic; valor.*

Creative – *originality in thought, expression and imagination; productive; imaginative; the quality of creating to cause something to come into being that is unique that would otherwise not naturally evolve through ordinary processes; to evolve one's own thought or imagination into a work of art or invention; to give rise to an occasion or person; to bring things about and cause to happen by intention or through design.*

Decisive, Decisiveness – *having the power or quality of making a decision; deciding; putting an end to controversy; characterized by displaying little to no hesitation; sure of one's self; indisputable; definite; commanding.*

Dedicated – *wholly committed to something or someone such as a goal or a cause or an activity; to devote wholly and earnestly to a purpose or a sacred purpose as in God; to set aside a specific task or function or purpose.*

Delighted – *to be highly pleased; captivated; enchanted; ecstatic.*

Determination, Determined – *the act of setting on a purpose or coming to a decision; ascertainment; solution; settlement of any dispute or question; the quality of being resolute and firmness of purpose or intention; settled.*

Devoted – *ardent in attachment, loyalty or affection; zealous; diligent; committed and loyal to a purpose, person, act or event.*

Diversified – *distinguished by variety; to invest in different types of securities, industries or activities; to balance assets and make diverse or widespread; Worldly.*

Dream – *an aspiration, goal or aim; a vision; a succession of images, thoughts or emotions passing through the mind while sleeping or an involuntary vision occurring while awake. To see an image in sleep or in a vision; a visualization, fancy or supposition. Imagination or devise.*

Empathetic – *the act of experiencing and understanding the thoughts, feelings or attitudes of another person as present in oneself.*

Empowered – *to feel enabled or permitted with the power or authority to capably accomplish something with strength and conviction.*

Energetic, Energized – *possessing energy in abundance, vitality, passion and effectiveness; to vigorously act; powerful forces; to rouse into activity; energize the spirit; to put forth effort.*

Evolving – *to develop gradually over time; to improve over time; to come forth and undergo transformation and improvement.*

Excellence, Excellent, Excelling – *the state of surpassing others or surpassing our own previous performance; to be superior in respect to an area, skill or talent; to be proficient; possessing outstanding quality; superior merit; extraordinary; remarkably good. Expert qualities.*

Expressive – *to be meaningful in the use of words, actions or phrasing; an indication of a feeling, spirit, character, quality; a look or intonation from a feeling; representation or power of an emotion, attitude or feeling.*

Extraordinary – *beyond the ordinary, usual or regular; exceptional. Special quality; brilliance; excellent.*

Fabulous – *incredible and almost impossible to believe; marvelous, superb; exceptionally good; excellent; admirable; special; wonderful.*

Faithfulness – *true to one's word, vows or promises; steady in allegiance; loyal; believers; the body of loyal members to a group or cause or faith; constant; reliable; trusted; believed; obsolete; adhering to fact, standard or account of an original; devoted.*

Fantastic – *appearing as if conceived by an unrestrained imagination; remarkable; odd; bizarre; fanciful; imaginary; marvelous; incredible.*

Fascinating – *being of great interest; enchanting; charming; captivating.*

Fortunate – *being of good fortune; lucky; blessed; favorable results.*

Funny – *providing fun; causing amusement or laughter; amusing; happy.*

Generous – *the act of being liberal in giving or sharing unselfishly; free from meanness; kind; abundant; magnanimous; ample.*

Gifted – *having great and special talent or ability; high intelligence; accomplished. Natural talent or ability.*

Glorious – *delightful; wonderful; enjoyable; brilliantly beautiful or magnificent; splendid.*

Grace, Graceful – *an elegance or beauty of one's manner or actions; pleasing quality or endowment; favor; goodwill; a virtue or excellence of divine origin. Also referred to as a state of Grace, the condition of being in God's favor.*

Grateful, Gratefulness – *deeply and warmly appreciative of kindness or benefit received' thankful' expression of gratitude; pleasing to the mind or senses; agreeable; welcome; refreshing.*

Great , Greatness – *wonderful; first rate; very good; being in an extreme or notable state; remarkable; exceptionally outstanding; high significance.*

Groovy – *slang for cool and highly stimulating; excellent; attractive.*

Happiness, Happy – *good fortune; pleasure; contentment; joy; the state of being happy; delighted or pleased; glad; characterized by contentment; favored by fortune; joyous; joyful; blissful; merry; successful; prosperous.*

Harmony – *a consistent orderly pleasing arrangement of parts; congruity; perfect combination of a structure or plan.*

Healthful, Healthy – *wholesome, conducive to good health; the general condition of the body or mind with reference to soundness and vigor; freedom of disease or ailment; vitality.*

Honest – *honorable in principles, intentions and actions; fair; upright; sincere; truthful; credible; humble; virtuous; integrity.*

Honorable – *in accordance with the principles of honor; dignity or distinction of high rank and respect; worthy of honor; highly respected; credible; distinguished.*

Honored – *honesty, fairness or integrity in one's actions or beliefs; a credible source or distinction; high respect, merit or rank; high esteem.*

Hope, Hopeful – *a feeling that what is wanted as an outcome will be a favorable finish; a particular feeling with regards to an expected outcome; to look forward to an outcome with a favorable desire with reasonable confidence; to believe, trust or desire; to feel positive that something desired or imagine will happen.*

Humbled – *modest; courteously respectful; complete absence of arrogance.*

Humility – *the quality of being humbled; modest opinion.*

Imaginative – *having exceptional powers of imagination; characterized by a fanciful imagination or creativity by forming mental images or concepts of what is not actually present to senses. A mental creation of images, a plan or an outcome.*

Incredible – *so extraordinary as to seem impossible; hard to believe real.*

Innovative – *the act of introducing new and different possibilities or methods; creative introduction of new things, concepts or ideas.*

Inspire, Inspiration – *the act of inspiring; exalting influence; to produce a feeling or thought upon another person; to communicate or suggest by a divine spirit; a divine influence directly and immediately exerted upon the soul and mind; the divine quality of the writing of words of spiritual influence. To give inspiration.*

Integrity – *the adherence to an ethical or moral principle; the state of being undiminished and whole; a sound, unimpaired condition of perfection; honesty.*

Intelligent – *possessing a good understanding with high mental capacity; comprehension of knowledge; quickness in understanding of thoughts, things or judgments; the faculty of having reason and understanding of a subject.*

Joy, Joyful, Joyous – *glad; delighted; an emotion of great delight or happiness caused by something exceptionally good or satisfying; a keen pleasure; the feeling of elation; felicity; happiness; rapture; bliss.*

Kind, Kindness – *a benevolent nature or disposition; considerate person; helpful; humane; gentle; calm; loving; good natured; gracious.*

Kindhearted – *a person that shows kindness or sympathy to another graciously or lovingly.*

Lovable – *of such a nature to attract love; amiable; endearing.*

Love – *a profound tenderness for another person' passionate affection; a feeling of warm personal attachment to another; an endearment; an enthusiasm of liking for anything; a concern for the well being of humanity; a benevolent affection of God and His creation.*

Loving – *the act of love; the feeling of love; the showing of love; warmly affectionate; fond.*

Loyal – *faithful; faithful to an oath, vow, commitment or obligation; loyal.*

Magnificent – *a splendid appearance; exceptional beauty; extraordinary; superb; noble; sublime; great; grand; lavish; fabulous.*

Meditation – *a continued or extended thought, reflection, contemplation or spiritual introspection. The act of meditating. To consider an intention, purpose or something to be done. To plan or contemplate in deep thought.*

Mindful – *to be attentive, aware or heedful; thoughtful; careful.*

Nurturing – *to encourage and support another during a learning, training or growing period; to feed and protect (as in a child); to foster growth and development; to educate.*

Organized – *to have a formal structure; systematize; to make neat and orderly; to clarify or plan; to be united.*

Passion, Passionate – *compelled, moved, or ruled by an intense emotion or strong feeling; influenced by emotions like love towards an experience.*

Patient – *calmly, quietly and steadily persevering through an activity or with another person without anger; displaying fortitude; bearing any annoyance or misfortune without complaint.*

Peace, Peaceful – *mutual harmony between people; freedom of the mind from annoyance, distraction, anxiety or obsession; tranquility; serenity; silence; stillness. A harmonic state of being.*

Perfection – *a quality or trait of the highest degree of proficiency, skill or excellence; the state of being and becoming perfect which is conforming to a definition of an ideal type; excellent beyond practical improvement; flawless; accurate; exact; thorough; correct in every detail; absolute.*

Plentiful – *abundant supply; yielding in great plenty or amount; richness.*

Positive – *explicitly expressed or stated in having no question; absoluteness; confident in fact or opinion; fully assured; non-speculative.*

Possibilities, Possible – *that something or someone may or can exist, happen or occur; that may be true which one has no knowledge to the contrary; feasible; practicable; chance; likelihood.*

Prayer – *a spiritual communion with God (or your higher power) in worship, thanksgiving, adoration, confession, plea, hope or devout petition*

Precious – *very valuable or costly; of great value; also highly esteemed for spiritual, nonmaterial or moral quality; beloved; dear; darling.*

Prepared – *ready, organized or well equipped; ready to be of service.*

Pretty – *attractive or pleasing to the eye as by delicacy or gracefulness without grandeur; pleasing to the ear, mind or aesthetic taste; fine; grand;*

Proactive – *anticipatory and prepared for an occurrence or event or activity; organized and in control of an expectation; ready to conquer situations.*

Prosperity, Prosperous – *flourishing, successful and thriving conditions; good fortune; abundance; favorable circumstances.*

Proud – *displaying or possessing a high regard and opinion of one's self, dignity and importance; feeling of high esteem and regard to oneself; highly gratifying to the feelings of self-respect and self-esteem; magnificent; majestic; full of vigor and spirit; brave; honorable; creditable.*

Pure – *simple or homogeneous and free from anything different from extraneous matter; unmodified; clear; free from blemishes; straightforward; unaffected; true; without discordant quality; free without guilt – guiltless; untainted, innocent; natural quality.*

Purposeful – having purpose; determined; significant; full of meaning.

Purpose – *the reason something truly exists or is made or is used or is complete; an intention of a desired result or outcome; end; aim; goal; determination; resolute; practical result or advantage; pure intention.*

Receptive – *willing to receive, take in or absorb ideas, knowledge, offers, suggestions, gifts. Open to accept truth.*

Refreshed – *to make fresh again; renew; invigorate; energize; restore; to provide new vigor and energy through rest or nourishment.*

Resourceful – *to skillfully and promptly deal with new situations or difficulties calmly with collective thought and organization using skills, talents and imagination.*

Respectful – *showing politeness, deference or courtesy to others; polite.*

Reverent – *deeply respectful attitude or feeling with awe; the outward manifestation of deep respect and admiration in awe.*

Shining - *a radiant, brilliant gleaming light; lustrous; outstanding; glistening; splendid; bright; eminent; distinguished.*

Sincere – *genuine; real; earnest; obsolete and unimpaired; free of deceit or falseness; pure.*

Smart – *quick and ready mental intelligence; shrewd, clever or witty mental capability; socially elegant; dashingly impressive or neat in appearance; fashionable; keen; prompt in action; readily effective.*

Special - *a character trait distinguishing what is ordinary or usual to extraordinary or exceptional; particularly valued; a particular distinction unique to a person or thing that brings about a specialty and pleasing difference or distinction.*

Spectacular – *dramatically daring or thrilling act, event or trait marked by an impressive distinction; impressive; elaborate; large scale display.*

Spirit, Spiritual, Spirituality – *Divine; a disposition or attitude in terms of vigor, courage, character, faith or divinity. Consisting of Spirit or soul as distinguished from the physical nature of being; incorporeal; close akin of like interests or outlooks; the immaterial nature of beings and things; the principle of conscious life animating the body or mediating between body and soul (incorporeal). The soul regarded as separate matter from a physical body in a conscious form; an angel, fairy, sprite or elf. Spirit is also an attitude or principle that inspires or pervades thoughts, feelings or actions. Holy Spirit is the third person of the trinity.*

Steadfast – *firmly grounded in position or purpose; resolute; faithful; firmly established or fixed in place.*

Success, Successful – *achieving or attaining success, position, honors or the like in a favorable endeavor; Outcome or result of prosperity from action taken towards a favorable quest.*

Sweet – *pleasing; amiable; precious; beloved; kind; gracious; fresh; nice.*

Thanksgiving – *the grateful acknowledgement of benefits or favors, especially to God. An expression of thanks or gratitude; a public expression or celebration of divine favor and kindness; graciousness; gratitude.*

The Light – *the source of an illumination; a beacon; radiance.*

Thoughtful – *a consideration of another; meditative; reflective; heedful; mindful; considerate.*

Trustworthiness, Trustworthy – *dependable; reliable; honest, fair; faithful; deserving of trust or the reliance of integrity, strength, confidence and surety.*

Truthful, Truthfulness - *trait or habit of conforming to complete honesty corresponding to reality or actual state of a matter; factual existence; a state of total integrity and truth in actual existence.*

Unique – *existing as the one and only sole characteristic and having no other equal or like; unparalleled; one true occurrence; a single outcome or result without an alternative possibility; an embodiment of a one given kind.*

Valued – *highly esteemed or regarded; cherished; having value.*

Victory – *a success or triumph; the ultimate position of achievement; a win.*

Virtuous – *conforming to moral and ethical principles; excellent; upright.*

Vision, Visionary– *an act or power of anticipation for what will come or may come to be; the act of seeing; sensing of the eyes; an experience whereby a person vividly and divinely sees an event, thing or personage in the mind although not actually physically present; a heavenly messenger; a vivid imaginative concept of anticipation.*

Vitality – *the exuberant physical strength and mental vigor; the power to live and grow; the capacity for survival or the continuation of a meaning or purposeful existence; a vital force – the force that perpetuates living beings, ideas and things to fruition.*

Vulnerable – *open to criticism, feedback or even being hurt – used here with the understanding that growth occurs with transparency and openness through being vulnerable or open.*

Warm-Hearted – *ability to show sympathy, affection, kindness, compassion through cordiality.*

Wealth, Wealthy – *an abundance of valuable possessions of anything (money, riches, joy, happiness, knowledge, etc) whether physical or spiritual; a great quantity; a plentiful amount; a state of prosperity; possessing wealth; affluence; rich in character, quality and ample abundance; wealth of insight and knowledge; wealth of Spirit; blessed*

A Note on Core Values …

Our individual and personal core values are the list of standards that have profound influence on our character, outlook, interpretation and attitude. These qualities are deeply etched into our mental and emotional blueprint and are not easily changed, thus require conscious acknowledgement and effort to evolve into a positive and purposeful core being. If there are qualities that you desire to have, focus on the meaning of the quality and embrace the acts or traits and characteristics associated with it.

Consider for a moment that your core values are like a navigation system or GPS. When you wander off course or lose direction, the system brings you back on track, and when you are fully clear on your core values, you can attract to you those like-minded people and situations that share the same desired path to lead a purposeful, authentic and fabulous life.

My Own Words, Virtues and Values

Here is a sacred space to add your own personal words, the virtues you may want to explore and any core values you would like to reflect upon or incorporate into your life ...

Fabulous

♥

**"Never worry about anything.
But in every situation let God know
what you need in prayers and requests
while giving thanks."**

- Philippians 4:6

Gratefulness

Acknowledgements

*I would like to acknowledge and recognize each of the originating authors, creators and contributors noted in **Reflections in Gratitude**. Thank you for sharing your wisdom, creativity and your endless dedication to excellence in your field of expertise and ultimately, thankfulness!*

A Course In Miracles

Saint Ambrose

Mitch Albom

Melody Beattie

Dr. Joyce Brothers

Carl W. Buechner

Buddha

Winston Churchill

Cicero

Walt Disney

Peter F. Drucker

Albert Einstein

George Elliston

Ralph Waldo Emerson

Epictetus

French Proverb

Benjamin Franklin

Audrey Hepburn

Clarence E. Hodges

Holy Bible NIV

Helen Keller

John F. Kennedy

Kevin Klimowski

C.S. Lewis

Doris Lessing

Joel Olsteen

Michael Rawls

Tony Robbins

Jim Rohn

Eleanor Roosevelt

Swami Sivananda

Success Coach Institute

Mother Teresa

David Henry Thoreau

Brian Tracy

Vietnamese Proverb

John Wanamaker

John Wooden

Yiddish Proverb

Zig Ziglar

❤

"Be transformed by the renewing of your mind."

- Romans 12:2

 Prayer

My Transformational

Moments of Fabulousness!

❤

Day/Date	Transformational Moments of Fabulousness!

Day/Date	Transformational Moments of Fabulousness!

Day/Date	Transformational Moments of Fabulousness!

Day/Date	Transformational Moments of Fabulousness!

Day/Date	*Transformational Moments of Fabulousness!*

Day/Date	Transformational Moments of Fabulousness!

About The Author

Jodi Nicholson is the Founder and CEO of A Fabulous Group, Inc. and Co-Founder and CEO of The Success Coach Institute. She is an Author, Speaker and Master Certified Success Coach specializing in life balance, business, marketing and motivation.

Combined with her entrepreneurial spirit and 25+ years of professional experience her passion for helping others to *live their most fabulous life* continues to flourish.

Whether coaching, consulting or training, Jodi consistently shows up smiling with her contagious enthusiasm that's sure to raise your spirits, bring more happiness to your life and inspire you to ...

Make It A Fabulous Day!

For more information about becoming one of Jodi's fabulous coaching clients, or to invite her to speak at your next event or conference, please contact:

A FABULOUS GROUP, INC.
3837 Northdale Blvd | Suite 328
Tampa, FL 33624 | USA

T: 813.217.3720 F: 813.960.8080

Jodi@AFabulousGroup.com
http://www.AFabulousGroup.com
http://www.JodiNicholson.com

Reflections in Gratitude – Order Form

NAME _____

ADDRESS _____

ADDRESS _____

CITY _____

STATE _____ ZIP _____

TELEPHONE _____

EMAIL _____

SEND _____ # Copies @ $ _____ Each = $ _____

MC Visa Discover _____

Expiration Date _____ 4 Digit Security Code _____

Signature _____

Plus applicable sales tax and shipping fees, add @$3.95 per book, Actual weight varies when ordering multiple copies and cost may increase or decrease slightly. All orders are verified prior to shipment. Phone orders are welcome by calling 1-888-689-1130.

Fax Orders: 813-960-8080

Email Orders: books@AFabulousGroup.com

Mail Orders: A Fabulous Group, Inc.
                3837 Northdale Blvd.
                Suite 328
                Tampa, FL 33624

Special Quantity Discounts

1-9 Books	$14.95 ea
10-99 Books	$12.95 ea
100-249 Books	$11.95 ea
250-499 Books	$10.95 ea
500-999 Books	$ 9.95 ea
1000+ Books	$ 8.95 ea

Thank You!